MONEY
WHAT IT IS
HOW IT WORKS

MONEY
WHAT IT IS
HOW IT WORKS

◆

Second Edition

*With a Plan for
Monetary Reform*

William F. Hummel

iUniverse, Inc.
New York Lincoln Shanghai

MONEY WHAT IT IS HOW IT WORKS
Second Edition

Copyright © 2007 by William F. Hummel

All rights reserved. No part of this book may be used or reproduced by any means, graphic, electronic, or mechanical, including photocopying, recording, taping or by any information storage retrieval system without the written permission of the publisher except in the case of brief quotations embodied in critical articles and reviews.

iUniverse books may be ordered through booksellers or by contacting:

iUniverse
2021 Pine Lake Road, Suite 100
Lincoln, NE 68512
www.iuniverse.com
1-800-Authors (1-800-288-4677)

The information, ideas, and suggestions in this book are not intended to render professional advice. Before following any suggestions contained in this book, you should consult your personal accountant or other financial advisor. Neither the author nor the publisher shall be liable or responsible for any loss or damage allegedly arising as a consequence of your use or application of any information or suggestions in this book.

ISBN-13: 978-0-595-42415-3 (pbk)
ISBN-13: 978-0-595-86751-6 (ebk)
ISBN-10: 0-595-42415-5 (pbk)
ISBN-10: 0-595-86751-0 (ebk)

Printed in the United States of America

Contents

Preface vii

Understanding Money

Money Basics 3
The Money Supply 7
Money as Credit 10
The Monetary Base 15
Some Common Misconceptions 21

The Banking System

Introduction to Banks 27
Non-Banks versus Banks 30
Bank Lending and Reserves 32
What are Eurodollars? 35
Foreign Exchange 39

Government Finance

Recycling Money 43
Government Debt versus Private Debt 47
Official Debt and Public Debt 50

Government "Trust Funds" 53
On Budget Deficits 56

More to Think About
Money and Inflation 61
Who Benefits from Seigniorage? 65
Tax or Borrow? 69
The Trade Deficit 72
Counterfeit Money, Who Takes the Hit?. 76

A Plan for Monetary Reform
The End of Fractional Reserve Banking...................... 81

About the Author 91

Preface

The essays in this book were selected from a much larger group that appears on my website at http://wfhummel.cnchost.com. They can be read in any order. However those unfamiliar with our monetary system will benefit by starting with the first section, **Understanding Money**.

Many books deal with money in relation to financial institutions and markets, but say little or nothing about the ***imperatives*** in a modern fiat money system. These essays should make it evident that conventional wisdom is encrusted with many misconceptions about the nature of money and how it works.

Most students of economics are taught that the Federal Reserve targets and controls the amount of bank reserves; that bank lending expands the money supply by a multiple of those reserves, depending on the required reserve ratio; that government borrowing causes interest rates to rise; that price inflation is normally caused by "too much money chasing too few goods." All of these are basically incorrect, yet they are often taken as axiomatic truths in economic analyses, with results that may go far astray from reality.

The literature is full of proposals for monetary reform, aimed at ending the fractional reserve banking system. However few explore the implications of fully-backed deposits in a fiat money regime. No modern nation has actually operated such a system, so we can't know with certainty how well it would work. The last essay in this book examines some of the key issues that must be addressed, and proposes a particular system.

Understanding Money

Money Basics

Money plays a central role in our lives, yet no one can be totally free of misconceptions about it. This article deals with only a few basic ideas, but it should help to gain an overall understanding of what money is and how it works.

Two Kinds of Money

Money is a token that is widely accepted as a medium of exchange. The token can be tangible like a coin or note, or intangible like a bank deposit. If the token is convertible on demand into a valuable commodity like gold, the token is known as ***commodity money***. The exchange value of commodity money varies, but is normally greater than its value as a commodity. A precious metal coin is simply a token potentially convertible into the bullion that comprises it.

If the tokens are intrinsically worthless and inconvertible, the government must endow them with a special status to make them viable as money. Such tokens are known as ***fiat money***. Except for collector's items, all government-issued tokens today are fiat money. One must therefore avoid thinking in terms of commodity money to understand modern money.

In the era of commodity money, the issuer was constrained by the need to hold a sufficient supply of the underlying commodity. There is no such constraint in the case of fiat money. The value of fiat money therefore depends on the policies and actions of the issuer, normally the central bank of a country. The remainder of this essay applies to the monetary system of the U.S. and not necessarily to other countries.

Fiat Money as a Tax Credit

The general acceptance of the government's fiat money derives from its status as legal tender and from the fact that it is required in payment of federal taxes. Those who have no tax liability have reason to acquire fiat money because it is of value to those who do. Thus fiat money can be viewed as a ***tax credit***, which will be used as a medium of exchange as long as the government widely enforces tax collection.

Base Money

Fiat money held by the private sector is known as the ***monetary base***, which we will refer to as ***base money***. The Fed issues base money when it buys securities from the public for its own portfolio, mainly Treasury debt. It pays by simply creating a deposit at the Federal Reserve Bank for the seller's own bank. This is known as ***monetizing the debt***.

Bank Money

Banks create deposits, known as ***bank money***, when they issue loans by simply crediting the borrower's account with a new deposit. The total amount of bank money increases when a bank issues a loan. When a loan is paid off, that amount of bank money vanishes.

The value of bank money is based on the promise that it can be converted on demand into base money at par. Current rules require a bank to hold ***reserves*** of base money equal to at least 10% of its transaction deposits. Reserves can be held in any combination of vault cash and deposit at the Fed. There is no required reserve for other bank liabilities, such as savings accounts or certificates of deposit.

Controlling the Price of Reserves

Even if there were no reserve requirement, a bank would have to hold enough reserves at the Fed to cover its depositors' checks, and enough vault cash to meet the demand for withdrawals by depositors. The need for reserves thus creates an active interbank market in which banks lend or borrow reserves among themselves. The interest rate on these short-term transactions is called the ***Fed funds rate.***

The Fed steers the Fed funds rate toward its target through its **open market operations**. These involve buying or selling securities in the open market to add or drain system reserves as needed to balance the supply and demand at its target for the Fed funds rate.

Any bank in good standing and with adequate collateral can borrow on a short-term basis at the Fed's ***discount window***. The interest rate the Fed charges is 100 basis points above its target rate for Fed funds. With that large a spread, the discount window is used by banks to cover temporary liquidity problems rather than as a source of reserves to back further lending.

The Fed's Reactive Role

Why does the Fed control the price of reserves rather than the quantity? The answer is that targeting the quantity risks endangering the liquidity of the banking system. For example, an increase in cash holdings by the public drains vault cash from the banking system. Unless the Fed responded by injecting reserves, one or more banks might be unable to meet either the reserve requirements or the withdrawal demands of its depositors.

Targeting the price of reserves is also more effective in controlling the volatility in the Fed funds rate, and thus the interest rate banks must charge on their loans. Firms cannot plan efficiently when the price of credit is subject to large and unpredictable variations.

As a result of the Fed's focus on price, the bank money supply will vary with demand. It expands or contracts according to whatever factors influence private sector borrowing. Thus the Fed plays an essentially reactive role, adding or draining reserves as needed for bank liquidity and to hold the Fed funds rate on target.

Limiting Bank Lending

Since the reserve ratio requirement doesn't really impede bank lending, what prevents a bank from responding to any and all loan demands? The answer is that every bank must also comply with an equity capital requirement. This is a complex formula that rates a bank's assets by risk, and requires that its capital exceed a certain fraction of its risk-weighted assets.

A bank can get into trouble by creating too many assets through lending. A bank with insufficient capital relative to its assets will be placed under supervision by its regulator who may then demand to approve any new lending.

Limiting Money Supply Growth

Another important question is what limits the bank money supply from growing excessively? Banks are in the business of selling credit. If a creditworthy borrower is willing to pay the bank's rate, the bank will normally make the loan even if it must borrow the required reserves after the fact. The only defense against the creation of an excessive supply of bank money is for the Fed to increase the price of reserves to the point that it slows net demand.

The Fed's basic monetary policy challenge is to keep the supply of bank money in reasonable balance with the needs of producers and the availability of goods and services. That calls for a great deal of knowledge about the economy as well as skill in interpreting the data. Mismanagement of the price of reserves can readily drive the economy off track towards inflation or recession. This is a difficult task, and the Fed has made its share of mistakes over the years that are usually obvious only in retrospect.

The Money Supply

What is meant by the ***money supply***? The term itself implies that a certain amount of money exists at any given time, even though the quantity may be unknown. In truth there can be no meaningful measure of the quantity because it is continually varying as a function of demand.

The Fed has its own arbitrary measures of the money supply which it once used to help guide its monetary policy decisions. It defines money as the total of cash in circulation and deposit liabilities of banks and thrifts. At one time it set targets for the growth of the money supply. Now it largely ignores its own measures because it has found little correlation between them and its major policy objectives—limiting inflation and unemployment.

Monetary Aggregates

The Fed has defined three monetary aggregates M1, M2, and M3. The narrowest definition, M1, includes the transaction deposits of banks and cash in circulation. M2 adds savings accounts, small time deposits at banks, and retail money market funds. M3 adds large time deposits, repurchase agreements, Eurodollars, and institutional money market funds. In March 2006 the Fed discontinued tracking M3 because it does not convey information about economic activity that is not already embodied in M2.

Note that the Fed's definition of the money supply includes only what the non-bank sector holds. Thus the reserves of banks, i.e. vault cash and deposits at the Fed, though a part of the monetary base, are not included in the monetary aggregates. That means when a bank spends for itself, it increases the money supply. When it receives payments from the public such as interest on loans, the money supply decreases.

Bank Lines of Credit as a Money Equivalent

An important shortcoming of the Fed's definition is that it ignores lines of credit which can be exercised at the discretion of the borrower. Firms often hold substantial lines of credit from their banks, which they can use on short notice. Likewise consumers hold lines of credit in their credit card accounts that are just as useful for purchases as checking accounts or the currency in their wallets. Lines of credit increase **liquidity**, which is ultimately what counts in terms of enhancing aggregate demand.

When someone uses a credit card in a purchase, he automatically expands the money supply. The seller receives a new deposit in his account, which increases the total of demand deposits in the banking system—until the buyer pays off the loan. The result is that consumers who roll over their credit card loans rather than paying them off have increased the money supply on their own initiative by hundreds of billions of dollars. In effect, the money supply is substantially larger and less measurable than the Fed's definition.

The Quantity Theory of Money

Economists regularly use the term **money supply** without defining it. A notable example is the equation of exchange in the quantity theory of money.

$$MV = PT$$

This relates the money supply, M, and the velocity of money, V, to the average price level, P, and the total number of transactions, T, in a given time period. The equation is simply an **identity**, meaning it is true by definition. Yet it is often used to "prove" that the average price level increases with the quantity of money. An identity says nothing about causal relations. The only thing we know is the product MV, which equals the national income, PT, which itself is only roughly measurable. The quantity of money, M, remains undefined and unknowable.

Money as Credit

Money does not exist in a pure **barter system**. Trades are negotiated by the participants as a fair exchange of goods and services. If someone agrees to receive equivalent value later in exchange for his goods, he has accepted an ***IOU***. An IOU is a credit for the seller and a debt for the buyer. If the IOU becomes negotiable, meaning others will accept it in exchange for goods and services, the IOU is money. In essence, **money is credit that is widely accepted as a medium of exchange**.

The Basic Properties of Money

An IOU will be accepted in exchange for goods and services only if it is seen as a store of value. However it does not have to store value indefinitely to qualify as money. It is money if it retains value long enough to be generally accepted as a medium of exchange. Money is always a store of value, but a store of value is not always money. For example, a bond is a store of value, but bonds are seldom accepted as a medium of exchange, and therefore are not money.

Most of the money we use is denominated in the unit of account established by the government. That enables us to measure the value of a good or service against another, based on what each sells for in the market. How many quarts of milk are equivalent in value to a barber shop haircut can only be determined in the market place.

IOUs as Money

Money is the credit side of a balance sheet relation. Every dollar of credit is matched by an equal amount of debt. A bank loan creates a credit for the borrower in the form of a ***negotiable IOU*** (the deposit) and a matching debt (the obligation to repay the loan). For the bank, it creates an often illiquid asset (the loan contract) and an equal liability (the negotiable IOU).

The term *money* is sometimes used in reference to high quality debt instruments nearing maturity. However such *near-money* is seldom acceptable as a medium of exchange. Besides being inconvenient to the seller, the monetary value of near-money is not really known until sold in the marketplace. The more restrictive definition of money will be adopted here.

Fed Funds and Bank Money

When the Fed purchases a financial asset from the public, it credits the seller's bank with a deposit at the Fed, known as **Fed funds**. Banks can exchange Fed funds for Federal Reserve notes, and vice versa, on demand. In either form, these Fed IOUs are the most negotiable in the economy. This is because the private sector must surrender Fed funds in paying Federal taxes. Conversely the government pays in Fed funds when it spends.

Individuals usually pay taxes with bank money, i.e. a check against a bank deposit. However the bank must cover the check with its own Fed funds. It cannot issue an IOU to cover the check. The Fed accepts bank money at par with its own IOUs. Thus bank deposits are nearly as negotiable in the private sector as Fed funds. Private party IOUs may be legally binding, but they are of uncertain monetary value and seldom negotiable. They are simply private debt rather than money.

Non-Bank Money

Money market mutual funds offer accounts similar to checking accounts at banks. They are actually shares in the ownership of short-term debt. When one pays with a draft on a money market fund, he is in fact selling shares in exchange for bank money that the fund must deliver. That means the fund must have sufficient bank money on hand, or acquire it through borrowing or sale of its own assets.

Although money market mutual funds are not insured or guaranteed to trade at par with Fed money, their acceptance is now so widespread that they have become de facto money. Thus ***non-bank financial institutions (NBFIs)*** can create money by selling an interest in short-term paper, and providing checking facilities against that paper.

Banks as Intermediaries

Like other intermediaries, banks borrow to lend at a profit. However banks are a special kind of intermediary because of their role as depositories. When a bank lends, it creates a new deposit to fund the loan and thus expands the money supply. It may issue loans only up to a prescribed multiple of its capital, and it must hold ***reserves*** of base money sufficient to cover net daily withdrawals of its depositors.

Reserves refer to a bank's vault cash and its Fed funds. Under present rules, a bank must hold 10% in reserves against its demand deposits, averaged over successive two-week periods. Averaging allows a bank to run below its required reserves on any given day. Interbank lending serves to redistribute reserves lost to other banks due to ordinary checking activities.

A bank can acquire Fed funds by borrowing in the money market, but it cannot increase its capital (assets minus liabilities) through borrowing. Banks with sufficient capital sometimes create new deposits without adequate reserves, and count on borrowing to meet the reserve requirement. That may leave the banking system short of reserves, and thus apply upward pressure on the interest rate in the Fed funds market. In order to defend its target interest rate, the Fed will supply the required reserves on its own initiative. Thus a net increase in credit issued by the banking system normally brings forth new base money.

Non-Banks as Intermediaries

Banks were once the main source of credit. Today NBFIs such as mutual funds, pension funds, finance companies, and insurance companies issue far more credit in total than do banks. Indeed, deposits created by banks now comprise less than 20% of the total credit market debt.

NBFIs are ordinary intermediaries that lend by transferring their own bank money to the borrowers. For example, NBFI **B** borrows $1 million from investor **A** at X%, and lends $1 million to entrepreneur **C** at Y%. In effect, $1 million in **A**'s bank account is transferred to **C**'s bank account. No new money is created, but the total credit market debt increases by $2 million. **B** expects to earn (Y-X)% on $1 million. **C** expects to profit from its loan, pay regular interest, and pay off its debt to **B** when it comes due. **B** will then have funds to pay off its debt to **A**.

What matters in this scenario is cash flow. Intermediaries typically borrow short to lend long, taking advantage of the normally upward sloping term structure of the *yield curve* (yield versus maturity). Such an intermediary must be able to roll over short-term debt on a continuing basis at favorable interest rates. If its credit standing is suspect, it may not be able it to borrow at all.

Cash flow also depends on factors over which the intermediary has no control. Suppose the Fed raised short-term rates sharply. Not only might **B** be in trouble due to the higher cost of rolling over its short-term debt, but **C** might also find its income reduced. If **C** were unable to service its debt, **B** might also fail, in which case **A** could lose a good part of its investment.

Systemic Risks

The Fed has virtually no control over the total amount of credit market debt. However the real danger to the financial system is not in how much credit is created. It is in the cascading of debt relations in which a single default can result in a system-wide reaction.

NBFIs are important players in a modern entrepreneurial economy, but they are not regulated as to their capital ratios or the type of assets they may hold. There is a constant danger of an over-leveraged NBFI having to default on a large debt. While the Fed or other financial institutions would likely come to the rescue, it is by no means certain that widespread havoc could be avoided under the rules that now exist.

The Monetary Base

Credit is the lifeblood of the economy. The amount and quality of credit market debt is a measure of the size and vitality of a nation's economy. All such debt rests like an inverted pyramid on a small foundation of money known as the ***monetary base***. The implicit assumption is that credit market debt is convertible at maturity into ***base money***.

The monetary base is the definitive money of a nation, meaning the State has no obligation to convert it on demand into some other form of money. The State defines the unit of account in base money, makes it ***legal tender for all debts, public and private***, and requires that payments to the State be in base money. In the following, we deal mainly with base money of the U.S.

A Brief History

During the era of gold as money, gold coins comprised the monetary base. The production of money was basically in the hands of the private sector. The State minted it or printed the certificates used in trade to represent it, while private enterprise mined the ore and reaped the benefits of doing so. The total amount produced was not under State control, but the relative scarcity of gold acted to maintain its exchange value at an acceptable level most of the time. The State had to acquire a share of the base money by levying taxes and fees on the public.

Today the monetary base is created in the form of inconvertible notes issued by the Federal Reserve, and bank credits at the Fed which can be exchanged for notes on demand. When the U.S. ended the use of gold for domestic currency in 1933, any constraint on the issue of base money was effectively removed. The State now has unlimited spending power in base money, and necessarily holds a monopoly on its issue.

Bank Credit and Base Money

A private enterprise with sufficient financial capital may obtain a charter that permits it to accept deposits of base money from the public, and to issue loans in the form of **credit** convertible to base money on demand. These depositories, commonly known as **banks**, must hold sufficient base money, called **reserves**, for that purpose.

When one deposits a check or cash in his account at a bank, he receives credit in exchange which we will refer to as **bank money**. We expect banks to redeem those credits for cash on demand.

Most of the money in use today exists as credits issued by private banks. However when one pays by drawing on his bank account, if the check is deposited in another bank, the payer's bank must transfer an equal amount of reserves to the payee's bank. Thus **base money is the foundation of the bank money system.**

Base Money as Credit

In reality, base money itself is a form of credit. In the same way a **contract** can be viewed as a **document** or the **agreement** it represents, **money** can be viewed as a **token** or the **credit** it represents. And since credit for the holder is debt for the issuer, money can also be viewed as a token representing **third party debt**. In the case of base money, the third party is the Fed.

All base money originates with the Fed. For the most part, it is issued in exchange for securities the public bought from the Treasury with base money previously acquired from the Fed. This circular system of credit is difficult for some to understand, especially for those who think of money only in terms of the token itself rather than the credit represented by the token.

If base money is simply a form of credit backed by Treasury securities, which are another form of credit, then what assures its viability as money, and what is the real basis of its value?

The Viability of Base Money

A token qualifies as money when it is widely accepted as a medium of exchange. To be accepted in that way, it must be seen as a ***store of value***, even though its value may decrease before its planned re-use. Notes and coins are convenient tokens because they are easy to use and reasonably durable. Bank deposits, which are claims on base money, can easily be transferred by wire to or from any bank. It remains to explain then why those tokens have value. Their status as legal tender in the discharge of debts is not sufficient because it says nothing about their value in ordinary use.

The viability of base money ultimately depends on the government enforcing tax collection, and acting to maintain a modest rate of price inflation. Base money acquires value because that is what the private sector must deliver in paying Federal taxes. Those who have no tax liabilities readily accept payment in base money because it is needed by so many others. ***In essence, base money is a tax credit***.

The Fed's base money liabilities are closely matched by its assets in the form of Treasury securities that it previously bought from the public. But what prevents the real value of those Treasury securities from being diluted by continued deficit spending? As will be explained, the purchasing power of base money has very little to do with the amount of deficit spending. However it does depend in the long run on the cost to banks of acquiring base money, which the Fed itself controls.

Fed Operations

Since base money is a monopoly of the State, the Fed must issue enough to avoid a shortage of what the public must use to pay its taxes. In practical terms, that means it must provide whatever reserves the banking system needs to ensure the liquidity of the payment system.

When the Fed needs to increase aggregate reserves, it buys Treasury securities from the public and credits the sellers' banks with additional deposits at the Fed. Conversely the Fed sells Treasury securities to the public from its own portfolio when it needs to decrease aggregate bank reserves. Bank reserves are only a small part of the monetary base, but they play a key role because they are the grease that enables the bank credit system to function.

These transactions by the Fed are designed to balance supply and demand for bank reserves at the Fed's target interest rate on overnight loans between banks, otherwise known as the **Fed funds rate**. The Fed funds rate is the benchmark for all short-term interest rates. It has a significant influence on the amount of bank money issued, and thus the liquidity of the private sector. In controlling the Fed funds rate, the Fed necessarily relinquishes control of the amount of base money it issues. The private sector itself determines the net amount issued.

Treasury Operations

The Treasury spends out of its account at the Fed. It continuously replenishes that account with transfers from its accounts in commercial banks where it deposits its receipts from taxes and the sale of bonds. These so-called **Treasury Tax and Loan** accounts in commercial banks are backed by deposits at the Fed, which are reserves of the banking system.

The Treasury simply recycles base money previously issued by the Fed. It approximately balances its receipts from taxes and the sale of bonds against its spending in order to avoid large variations in the demand deposits of the private sector which could significantly affect liquidity. It targets a fixed balance in its account at the Fed in order to minimize variations in the aggregate reserves of the banking system. The Fed compensates for the variations by adding or draining reserves on a short-term basis through its **open market operations**.

If the private sector holds more base money than it needs, it will normally use the excess to purchase interest-earning Treasury securities, since base money earns no interest. Thus the Treasury will always be able to recapture its deficit spending through the sale of securities, since it can pay whatever interest the market demands.

Managing Inflationary Expectations

The interest rate the Treasury must pay to borrow is a market rate which is influenced by Fed policy. The short-term rate closely tracks the Fed funds rate due to arbitrage. Longer-term rates include a premium over the Fed funds rate which varies with inflationary expectations. Although many diverse factors affect those expectations, the Fed itself has considerable influence through its monetary policy decisions.

It is therefore up to the Fed to keep inflationary expectations within acceptable limits. By doing that well, it protects the purchasing power of base money, and ensures that interest rates on long term borrowing will not become so burdensome as to prevent economic growth.

Contrary to conventional wisdom, the historical record shows no significant correlation between the amount of deficit spending and the inflation rate or interest rates. Most central banks now target a small positive inflation rate to provide a margin against a ***deflation trap***. Deflation hurts aggregate demand by creating a money-hoarding psychology which is difficult to overcome, and may result in a prolonged recession. Under the gold-based system, the State's ability to counter inflationary and deflationary pressures was very limited.

In Summary

Base money is simply another form of credit. The Fed issues base money in exchange for credits issued by the Treasury which the public previously bought with base money. This circular system of credit works as long as the State broadly enforces tax collection. Price inflation varies in the short run for a number of reasons not directly under the control of the State. In the long run, Fed policy in setting the cost to banks of acquiring base money is the key to controlling the average inflation rate.

Some Common Misconceptions

Where does all the money go when stock prices plummet?

This question mistakes the monetary value of stocks for money itself. Stock prices simply reflect the current market value of the shares. At the end of the day, buyers own more shares and less money, while sellers own fewer shares and more money. Their aggregate financial wealth may be higher or lower, but the total amount of money they own remains unchanged in these transactions.

The government causes inflation when it prints too much money.

Money is literally printed by the government only to meet the demand for portable currency, i.e. Federal Reserve notes. The notes are issued to banks in exchange for deposits the banks hold at the Fed. The public acquires the notes in exchange for their own deposits at banks. The amount of currency issued is no more and no less than the public desires to hold as wallet money or rainy day money. It has no bearing on inflation.

Price inflation is mainly caused by too much money chasing too few goods.

This reflects a misunderstanding about how the money supply grows in a modern money system. Money exists mainly in the form of bank deposits, created when banks issue loans. Money growth thus depends on the demand for bank loans and the willingness of banks to lend. The Fed can influence the demand through its control of the interest rate, but it does not directly control the amount of bank lending. If the Fed sets the interest rate too low for an extended period, the amount of bank money could grow enough to put upward pressure on prices. That mainly affects asset prices, but is seldom the cause of consumer price inflation.

Banks lend the money of their depositors.

When banks issue loans, they create new deposits without disturbing existing deposits. That is precisely what causes the money supply to grow, and is what distinguishes bank lending from all other types of lending. A non-bank intermediary like a finance company lends what it has on deposit at a bank. It cannot create new deposits as a bank is able to do.

The money multiplier explains how much money banks can create.

The money multiplier has no predictive power. It is simply an after-the-fact observation of the ratio between aggregate demand deposits and banking system reserves. A bank's lending is constrained by its capital adequacy, not its reserves.

Bank reserves ensure that funds will be available for withdrawals by depositors.

Minimum reserve requirements on banks were once viewed as a protection for depositors. Many countries now impose no reserve requirement on their banks. Banks must hold sufficient reserves to cover withdrawals by depositors. But a solvent bank that is temporarily short of reserves can borrow them from the central bank or in the money market. Indeed a bank can hold ample reserves and still be insolvent. Protection for depositors against default is provided by deposit insurance, not by the reserves of the banks.

Government deficit spending increases the money supply.

Deficit spending increases the net financial wealth of the private sector in the form of Treasury securities, not money. Every dollar the Treasury spends is money previously created by the Fed. The Treasury simply recycles the money it acquires from taxes and the sale of securities. In the aggregate, the public pays for Treasury securities out of the funds acquired from the deficit spending itself.

The Fed controls the size of the money supply.

A bank in the U.S. must hold reserves of base money in proportion to the amount of its demand deposit liabilities. However the amount a bank may lend is limited by its own capital, not its reserves. In order to maintain control of the Fed funds rate, i.e. interbank lending rate, the Fed must provide whatever reserves are required by the banking system as a whole. In fact if the Fed withheld reserves, it could imperil the liquidity of one or more banks. Thus for all practical purposes, the Fed cannot even control the amount of base money it issues.

Government borrowing drains loanable funds needed within the private sector.

The government does not borrow to accumulate funds in the Treasury. It borrows only to cover its deficit spending, and thus does not affect the size of the private sector money supply on average. While government borrowing could temporarily reduce the supply of loanable funds within the private sector, that effect is short-lived and typically negligible.

Interest paid on the debt reduces the funds available for other government spending.

There is no basic constraint on government spending in its own currency. Interest payments and the revenues that support them are part of the balanced reciprocal flow of funds between the Treasury and the private sector. Their only effect is a redistribution of financial assets, which of course is true of all government spending.

The Banking System

Introduction to Banks

The bulk of all money transactions today involve the transfer of bank deposits. Depository institutions, which we normally call **banks**, are at very the center of our monetary system. Thus a basic knowledge of the banking system is essential to an understanding of how money works.

Bank Deposits and Reserves

The *monetary base* is created by the Fed when it buys securities for its own portfolio. Bank deposits themselves are not *base money*, rather they are claims on base money. A bank must hold *reserves* of base money in order to meet its depositors' cash withdrawals and to cover the checks written against their accounts. Reserves comprise a bank's vault cash and what it holds on deposit at the Fed, known as *Fed funds*. The Fed requires banks to maintain reserves of at least 10% of their *demand deposits*, averaged over successive 14-day periods.

The Movement of Bank Reserves

When a depositor writes a check against his account, his bank must surrender that amount in reserves to the payee's bank for the check to clear. Reserves are constantly moving from one bank to another as checks are written and cleared. At the end of the day, some banks will be short of reserves and others long. Banks redistribute reserves among themselves by trading in the Fed funds market. Those long on reserves will normally lend to those short. The annualized interest rate on interbank loans is known as the *Fed funds rate*, and varies with supply and demand.

The reserve requirement applies only to the bank's demand deposits, not its term or savings deposits. Thus when a bank depositor converts funds in a demand deposit into a term or savings deposit, he frees up the reserves that were held against the demand deposit. The bank can then use those reserves in several ways. For example, it can hold them to back further lending, buy interest-earning Treasury securities, or lend them to other banks in the Fed funds market.

Controlling the Fed Funds Rate

The ***supply*** of reserves changes whenever base money enters or leaves the banking system. This occurs when the Fed buys or sells securities or when the public deposits or withdraws cash from banks. The ***demand*** for reserves changes whenever total demand deposits change, which occurs when banks increase or decrease aggregate lending. The Fed controls the Fed funds rate by adjusting the supply of reserves to meet the demand at its target interest rate. It does so by adding or draining reserves through its ***open market operations***.

The Fed funds rate effectively sets the upper limit on the cost of reserves to banks, and thus determines the interest rates that banks must charge the public for loans. Bank interest rates influence the demand for loans, and thereby the net amount of bank lending. That in turn determines the liquidity of the private sector, which is important in terms of aggregate demand and inflationary pressures. The selection and control of the Fed funds rate is the key monetary policy instrument of the Fed.

The Effects of Government Spending

The Fed acts as a depository for the Treasury as well as member banks. All government spending is paid out of the Treasury's account at the Fed. Whenever the government spends, the Fed debits the Treasury's account and credits the Fed account of the payee's bank. The Treasury replenishes its Fed account with transfers from its commercial bank accounts where it deposits the receipts from taxes, and the sale of its securities.

In order to minimize variations in aggregate banking system reserves, the Treasury maintains a nearly constant balance in its Fed account. In effect,

Treasury payments are simply transfers from its commercial bank accounts to the bank accounts of the public. Funds move in the reverse direction when the public pays taxes or buys securities from the Treasury. The Treasury must maintain a positive balance in its commercial bank accounts to avoid having to borrow directly from the Fed. However it has no need for, and does not accumulate, balances in excess of its near-term payment obligations.

On average, government spending does not affect the aggregate bank deposits of the private sector. The Treasury sells or redeems securities as required to balance its inflows against outflows. However short-term variations occur because receipts cannot be synchronized with spending. Banking system reserves remain essentially unaffected by government spending because the Treasury transfers funds from its commercial bank accounts to replace the funds spent out of its Fed account.

Non-Banks versus Banks

Banks play a key role in the monetary system, yet their lending now accounts for less than 20% of the total credit market debt in the U.S. Most of the lending is done by non-bank financial institutions such as finance companies, mortgage companies, insurance companies, pension funds, and investment banks. Non-banks cannot accept demand deposits, and therefore play no direct role in the payment system. But they provide a variety of financial products and compete with banks and each other for lending opportunities.

Non-Bank Lending

Non-banks are ordinary intermediaries. They act as a conduit between those with funds to lend and those in need of funds. By pooling the funds of investors from whom they borrow, they can then lend in various amounts and periods. For their service they charge a fee, usually in the form of periodic interest payments. Their borrowing and lending increases the total credit market debt but has no direct effect on the money supply. Non-banks simply *intermediate* the transfer of funds from the bank accounts of the original investors to the bank accounts of the ultimate borrowers.

Non-banks usually borrow short-term at lower rates to lend longer term at higher rates. That means a non-bank must be able to roll over its short-term debt at favorable rates. It must also be able to borrow on short notice to manage any cash flow problem. For that reason it must maintain an excellent credit rating, or it may not be able to borrow at all.

Bank Lending

Banks are not ordinary intermediaries. Like non-banks, they also borrow, but they do not lend the deposits they acquire. They lend by crediting the borrower's account with a new deposit, and then if necessary borrowing the funds needed to meet the reserve ratio requirement. The accounts of other depositors remain intact and their deposits fully available for withdrawal. Thus a bank loan increases the total of bank deposits, which means an increase in the money supply. When the loan is paid off, the money supply decreases.

A net increase in bank lending results in a shortage of reserves needed by the banking system, which only the Fed can supply. In order to maintain control of the Fed funds rate, i.e. the interest rate on overnight loans between banks, the Fed must provide the funds as required. It does so by purchasing Treasury securities from the public.

Bank lending has no effect on a bank's own capital. But bank lending is limited by the capital ratio requirement set by the Fed. If a bank has sufficient capital, it can expand its balance sheet by issuing more loans. However if it is not holding excess reserves, it will have to acquire more in order to meet the reserve ratio requirement. Banks therefore actively seek new deposits. Of course they prefer deposits on which they pay no interest, like ordinary checking accounts. They also borrow from savers who open savings accounts and investors who buy their CDs.

Bank Lending and Reserves

The following scenario illustrates how the reserve ratio requirement relates to bank lending. Suppose a bank has $100,000,000** in demand deposits and $10,000,000 in reserves, which is just enough to meet the reserve ratio of 10%. The bank plans to issue mortgage loans totaling $5,000,000 for a new housing development. Can it do so before it acquires more reserves? [** The reserve ratio required for that amount of demand deposits is somewhat less than 10%, but we use that figure to keep the arithmetic simple.]

Capital Adequacy Requirement

A bank's lending is ultimately limited by the amount of its own capital (assets minus liabilities). The capital adequacy rule requires that the ratio of its capital to risk-weighted assets be at least 8%. Mortgage loans have a risk weighting of 0.5 in contrast to ordinary loans which have a risk weighting of 1.0. Since the bank plans to expand its balance sheet by $5,000,000, it must have excess capital of at least $5,000,000 x 0.5 x .08 = $200,000. We will assume the bank satisfies this requirement.

Borrowing Reserves when Needed

Assume the first loan is for $1,000,000. The immediate effect of the loan is to increase the bank's assets and liabilities by that amount, without affecting its reserves or capital. When the borrower spends the $1,000,000, if the proceeds are deposited in other banks, the lending bank loses that much in reserves to other banks but it no longer has that deposit liability. However the bank's original demand deposits of $100,000,000 have not changed, and they are now backed by only $9,000,000 in reserves. The bank must therefore acquire $1,000,000 more in reserves to meet the 10% reserve requirement.

Other banks now have $1,000,000 in new deposit liabilities, as well as new reserves of the same amount. Since they only need $100,000 of those reserves to back their new deposits, they could use the remaining $900,000 to back additional lending of their own. But let's assume they have no good lending opportunities at the time, and therefore offer to lend the excess reserves in the Fed funds market. The lending bank could borrow the excess reserves, which would still leave it $100,000 short of what it needs. Where will the extra funds come from?

How the Fed Responds

Other things equal, aggregate demand deposits of the banking system have increased by $1,000,000, but aggregate reserves remain unchanged. The banking system will thus be short $100,000 of what is needed for all banks to meet their reserve requirements. This shortage applies upward pressure on the Fed funds rate, which will bring a response from the Fed's open market operation.

The Fed will purchase $100,000 of Treasury securities from the public, thereby injecting what is needed to restore the balance and hold the Fed funds rate on target. The full $1,000,000 that the bank needs will therefore be available to borrow in the Fed funds market, and at an interest rate close to the target Fed funds rate. Of course the actual scenario is not as neat and precise as this, but we are only seeking to understand the principle.

Issuing the Remaining Loans

This process can be repeated with other borrowers to issue the $5,000,000 in new mortgage loans. The Fed will then have added $500,000 to banking system reserves on its own initiative. At no time has the reserve requirement been a constraint on the bank's lending. Assuming it has a good credit rating, the bank can borrow the reserves as needed. Indeed it can do so after each loan has been issued because reserves are figured as the average over successive fourteen day periods. That allows a bank to be short of reserves on any given day.

Maintaining Control of the Fed funds rate

We have assumed that the money loaned by the bank and spent by the borrowers has all remained in demand deposits around the banking system. If instead some of that money gets parked in savings or term deposits for which reserves are not required, the banking system would likely have more reserves than it needed and would offer them in the Fed funds market. In order to hold the Fed funds rate on target, the Fed would need to drain the excess reserves. It would do so by selling Treasury securities from its own portfolio.

Note that the whole system revolves around what must be done to control the Fed funds rate, the primary monetary policy tool of the Fed. The Fed funds rate sets the upper limit on the cost to banks of borrowed funds, which in turn determines the interest rate banks charge on loans to the public.

What are Eurodollars?

Many foreign banks as well as foreign branches of U.S. banks accept deposits of U.S. dollars and grant the depositor an account denominated in dollars. Those dollars are called **Eurodollars**. As we will see, they exist under quite different constraints from domestic dollars. While Eurodollar banking got its start in Europe, such banking is now active in major financial centers around the world.

Importance of Eurodollars

Today the Eurodollar market is the international capital market of the world. It includes U.S. corporations funding foreign operations, foreign corporations funding foreign or domestic operations, and foreign governments funding investment projects or general balance-of-payment deficits.

Overseas branches of a U.S. bank are treated as an integral part of the parent bank. In its published statements the parent bank consolidates the assets and liabilities of all branches, domestic and overseas, and it has just one account at the Fed, held by the head office. However each overseas branch keeps its own books for day-to-day operations.

An Example

Suppose the AAA Corporation draws a check for five million dollars on Citibank, its New York bank, and deposits it at a London Eurodollar bank. The result is that the ownership of five million U.S. dollars has passed from AAA to the London bank in exchange for a Eurodollar time deposit. The London bank now holds a deposit at Citibank balanced by a liability, the time deposit credited to AAA.

Since that money earns no interest at Citibank, the London bank will use the funds to make a loan, say to the BBB Corporation which banks at Wells Fargo. Citibank will then show a decrease of five million dollars on deposit at the Fed and a decrease in liability of that amount to the London bank. Wells Fargo will gain that deposit at the Fed and an equal liability as a deposit for BBB. The London bank will record a loan of five million dollars to BBB balanced by a time deposit owed to AAA.

Eurodollars Never Leave the U.S.

Regardless of where they are deposited, London, Bahrain, or Singapore, and regardless of who owns them, Americans or foreigners, Eurodollars never leave the U.S. Note that throughout both transactions there was no change in banking system reserves at the Fed, and the $5 million remained on deposit at a U.S. bank. A somewhat more involved analysis would show this to be true even if the Eurodollars had been lent to a foreign corporation.

In this example, the London eurobank is acting as a financial intermediary in U.S. dollars. It is doing much the same as any U.S. non-bank intermediary, like a finance company or a pension fund. ***Unlike domestic U.S. banks, Eurobanks cannot create money in U.S. dollars through the act of lending. Their lending only transfers ownership of deposits at U.S. banks.***

Eurobanking Practices

Banking ground rules in the Euromarket differ sharply from those in the U.S. domestic arena. One important distinction is in the character of their liabilities. In the Euromarket, all deposits with the exception of call money have a fixed maturity that may range from one day to five years. Also, interest is paid on all deposits, the rate being determined by market conditions.

For U.S. banks, another important distinction between their domestic and Euro operations is that no reserve requirements and no FDIC premiums are imposed against their Eurodollar deposits. Thus they can invest every Eurodeposit they receive. The Euromarket operates outside the control of any central bank.

Eurobank Investments

Banks accepting Eurodollar deposits use the dollars to make two sorts of investments, **loans** and **interbank placements**. All such placements, like other Eurodeposits, have fixed maturities and bear interest. The rate at which banks in London offer Eurodollars in the placement market is referred to as the London interbank offered rate, **LIBOR** for short.

The usual practice is to price loans at LIBOR plus a spread. Some term loans are priced for the life of the loan, but far more often they are priced on a rollover basis. This means that every three or six months, the loan is re-priced at the prevailing LIBOR for 3-or 6-month money plus the agreed-upon spread.

Source of Eurodollar Funds

The funds that form the basis for the Eurodollar market are provided by a wide range of depositors: large corporations (domestic, foreign, multinational), central banks and other government bodies, supranational institutions such as the Bank for International Settlements, and wealthy individuals. Most of the funds come in the form of time deposits with fixed maturities.

The Eurobanks also receive a certain amount of call money. A call account can be a same-day value account, a 2-day notice, or a 7-day notice account. The going rate for call money closely tracks the overnight Eurodollar rate, which in turn is tied by active arbitrage to the U.S. Fed funds rate. The main attraction of a call deposit is liquidity. Time deposits pay more, but a penalty is incurred if such a deposit is withdrawn before maturity.

Lender of Last Resort

Two questions arise regarding the liquidity of the Euromarket: Who lends if the supply of Eurodollars dries up? Who lends if the solvency of a major bank in the Euromarket is threatened? The dollars don't disappear, but it's possible that holders of Eurodollar deposits could move them back to banks in New York. Thus Eurobanks could face a liquidity crisis. To protect against any such risk, many have negotiated standby lines with U.S. banks.

In addition, central banks have concluded that each looks after its own. Thus the Fed is the appropriate lender to a U.S. banker whether its troubles arise from its New York or London operations. Other central banks are expected to stand behind their own domestic banks both at home and abroad.

Foreign Exchange

Payment involving the transfer of bank deposits from the buyer's account to the seller's account is very simple if both buyer and seller share the same bank. The process is only a little more complex when they have different banks if both banks are part of the same clearing system. If the two banks are in different clearing systems, payment is substantially more complex.

A Case of Different Clearing Systems

Consider a U.S. importer who buys a shipment of Swiss watches. Assume the exporter requires payment in francs to his account at a Swiss bank, which of course is in a different clearing system. Normally the importer will go to the foreign exchange desk of his own bank and pay the dollars required to buy the francs as a deposit in a Swiss bank. The details of this transaction are handled by his own bank. A check can then be drawn on the Swiss bank in payment to the exporter. When the exporter deposits the check in his Swiss bank, it will clear in the normal fashion through the Swiss banking system.

Where does the U.S. bank get the Swiss francs to sell to the importer? If the bank is large enough and does business in foreign exchange, it may maintain a deposit of its own at a Swiss bank. If not, it can buy the francs in the interbank market in foreign currencies where the ownership of deposits in different currencies is traded. Small banks may need the services of a correspondent bank that has trading facilities.

Use of a Forward Contract

If the importer's payment is not due for say three months, he can buy a forward contract with his bank for delivery of francs at that time. This locks in the dollar price and thus protects him against changes in the exchange rate before actual payment is required. If the amount were large enough, the bank would hedge its own risk with a currency swap in the foreign exchange market.

A currency swap consists of two simultaneous transactions. In this example, one would be the purchase of francs for dollars for immediate delivery in the *spot market*. The other would be a contract in the *forward market* allowing the bank to sell francs for dollars at an agreed upon price three months hence. At that time the francs would be delivered as required. The currency swap locks in the exchange rate and thus protects the bank. The bank makes its profit as a markup in the forward contract bought by the importer.

The Foreign Exchange Market

Because so much of world trade is conducted directly in US dollars, foreign exchange between non-U.S. currencies usually involves conversion into and out of U.S. dollars. The foreign exchange market is an international market, active around the clock. London has by far the largest market, followed by New York, Tokyo, and Singapore. Large banks and security dealers maintain trading rooms where they post on computer screens around the world their bid and ask prices for currencies relative to the U.S. dollar. Quotes are offered for both the spot market and the forward market.

Foreign exchange trading has grown rapidly since 1971. That is the year Nixon ended gold backing for the U.S. dollar in international payments, thus leaving the exchange rates of the world's currencies to float at market prices. The volatility of those rates has increased dramatically since the mid-1970s, creating investment risk as well as opportunities for speculative gain. Foreign exchange trading in support of commerce is now just the tip of the iceberg, probably less than 5% of the total.

Government Finance

Recycling Money

This article traces money flows within the U.S. We deal with two types of money, **base money** and **bank money**, and focus on how they move between the **public**, the **banks**, the **Fed**, and the **Treasury**.

The **public** comprises firms and households, which are the producing and consuming sectors of the economy. **Banks** comprise the depositories which provide payment services as well as financial intermediation for the public.

Base Money

The **monetary base** is the definitive money of the nation. It exists in two forms (1) notes and coins issued by the Fed, and (2) deposits of banks at the Fed. Both are referred to here as **base money**, and are interchangeable on demand. The Fed has sole authority for issuing base money. It does so by purchasing Treasury securities for its own portfolio, and crediting the seller's bank with a deposit at the Fed. This is known as **monetizing the debt**. Conversely when the Fed sells securities, that amount of base money vanishes.

Although base money is not a claim on any Fed assets, it is carried as a liability on the Fed's balance sheet, backed by the financial assets it has purchased. In principle, those assets could include corporate bonds and stocks. In practice, the Fed acquires only Treasury securities because of their liquidity and credit-worthiness. The Fed issues only non-interest-earning liabilities.

Bank Money and Bank Reserves

Banks issue credit when they accept deposits and when they create new deposits to fund loans. A bank checking deposit is simply a promise to deliver base money on demand. Since bank deposits can be easily transferred by check or electronic means, they serve as a medium of exchange, and therefore as money.

A bank's reserves comprise its deposit at the Fed, known as **Fed funds**, plus its vault cash. Any payment involving the transfer of deposits between banks requires an equal transfer of Fed funds between the respective banks. When one writes a personal check to make a purchase, the bank's account at the Fed is debited to cover the check. That means a bank must have **reserves** of base money in order to do business. In the special case when the check is deposited in the same bank on which it is drawn, only a transfer of deposits within the bank is involved.

Bank reserves comprise a small fraction of the monetary base, but they play a key role. The Fed adds or drains reserves as required to balance the supply and demand at its target Fed funds rate. Aggregate reserves increase when the Fed buys Treasury securities from the public and decrease when it sells Treasury securities. The public also affects aggregate reserves when it deposits or withdraws cash from banks, causing the Fed to rebalance reserves to compensate for changes in aggregate vault cash.

When the Fed needs to adjust banking system reserves, it deals with a group of financial institutions known as **primary dealers** comprising banks and securities dealers. It does not concern itself with individual banks needing reserves. Banks short of reserves have to borrow them in the money market or in the Fed funds market from those long on reserves. They can also borrow from the Fed, but only at a penalty rate above the Fed funds target rate.

The Transaction Money Supply

The Fed has defined a measure of the transaction money supply and named it **M1**. It consists of (1) cash in circulation, (2) travelers checks, and (3) demand deposits at commercial banks, but not the deposits of other banks, the US government, and foreign central banks. Note that the money supply comprises only *liabilities* of the Fed and the banking system. Reserves are bank *assets*, and not a part of the money supply.

Although cash is the ultimate form of money, by dollar volume it plays a minor role in the economy. Cash and traveler's checks are used mainly as portable money in retail purchases. The largest volume of transactions by far involves the transfer of bank deposits, i.e. bank money.

M1 reflects the demand for liquidity (immediate spending power) by the private sector. The demand increases with inflation and varies with economic conditions. For example, during recessions both firms and households spend less, so they usually move some of their demand deposits into savings vehicles like T-bills and CDs.

Of the many factors that influence M1, the most significant is the demand for Federal Reserve notes which has been steadily growing. Most of that demand comes from overseas, but the increasing immigrant population in the US is also an important factor. As more notes are withdrawn from banks, the Fed must buy more Treasury securities from the public to prevent a drain on banking system reserves. This effect is seen most clearly in the steady growth of Treasury securities in the Fed's portfolio.

Treasury Operations

The Treasury deposits its receipts from taxes and the sale of its securities in commercial bank accounts, known as ***Treasury Tax and Loan (TT&L)*** accounts. Like ordinary bank accounts, TT&L accounts are bank money but are not a part of M1 because they are owned by the government.

The Treasury pays its bills out of its account at the Fed. Those payments transfer base money into the banking system. Since that would increase aggregate banking system reserves, the Treasury simultaneously transfers funds from its TT&L accounts to its Fed account which reduces banking system reserves. By targeting a constant balance in its Fed account, it minimizes disturbances to banking system reserves and thereby facilitates the Fed's control of the Fed fund rate. Thus *for all practical purposes, the Treasury spends out of its commercial bank accounts*.

The Treasury has no use for, and does not accumulate, funds in its TT&L accounts in excess of its near-term payment obligations. On average it balances inflows against outflows by selling or redeeming its securities, as required. Deficit spending is covered by the net sale of securities to the public. In the aggregate, the funds the public spends to buy those securities come from the deficit spending itself. Thus, except for short-term transients, the private sector's bank money supply is not affected by Treasury transactions.

Government Debt versus Private Debt

To understand the difference between government debt and private debt, we must first understand the distinct roles played by base money and bank money. This distinction is of little significance to the average person, but it is of crucial importance to the banking system.

Why the Government Borrows

When we adopted a monetary base of intrinsically worthless paper money in the mid-20th century, we created a new paradigm that is still widely misunderstood. The imperatives are quite different from those of the earlier gold-based system. The key to maintaining the purchasing power of money is to control the price of credit. That means controlling the cost to banks of acquiring the reserves of base money they need to back their lending. It is up to the Treasury and Fed acting together to do that, and Treasury plays an indispensable role.

The public borrows from banks in order to acquire transaction deposits (bank money) to spend on investment or consumption. In contrast, the government borrows from the public simply to recapture its deficit spending, all of which is base money. It does so to enable the Fed to control the supply of reserves in the banking system, and thereby control the short-term interest rate. The ultimate objective is to control the inflation rate over the long term.

Rolling Over Government Debt

Nothing about government debt in a fiat money system requires that it be paid off. Of course individual securities must be redeemed as they mature, but the Treasury can roll over its maturing debt indefinitely. Rolling over means selling new securities to pay for the redemption of maturing securities. This involves no new tax revenues.

Treasury securities offer a risk-free, interest-earning alternative to base money spent into circulation by the government. If the private sector has more non-interest-earning base money in the aggregate than it wishes to hold, its only alternative is to buy Treasury securities. Since the Treasury can pay whatever interest rate the market demands, there will always be willing buyers of its securities.

Government Debt as Perpetuities

The debt can be carried indefinitely at no financial risk to either the government or the private sector. Individuals can become bankrupt with too much borrowing, but the government can never become bankrupt if it borrows in the same currency it issues.

Government debt is commonly regarded as a future tax liability of the private sector. However the unique position of the government as issuer of the monetary base enables it to roll over its debt continuously. In doing so, its securities become the functional equivalent of perpetuities, i.e. bonds that never mature and thus are never redeemed. De facto, there can be no net tax liability on perpetuities.

Net Financial Wealth of the Private Sector

Treasury securities are valuable assets for the holders. They can readily be sold for money or pledged as collateral for loans. Together with the monetary base they comprise the ***net financial wealth*** of the private sector. By contrast, bank lending does not affect the financial wealth of the private sector because all such credit is matched by an equal amount of borrower debt.

The value of the Treasury securities to the private sector as a whole is not in the interest payments they shed. Those payments are matched by tax revenues, and are therefore a wash in the aggregate. The value is in the principal, just as in the case of Federal Reserve notes. They represent stored financial wealth for the holder. The public trades one for the other, depending on the degree of liquidity it desires at any given time.

The Upper Limit to Government Debt

If the net financial wealth of the private sector is allowed to grow too large, the penalty could be price inflation, even though the amount of base money remains unchanged. This is due to the "wealth effect" on consumer spending. But as long as the private sector treats government securities as a savings vehicle, it is benign and a valuable asset for the nation.

The debt/GDP ratio reached an all-time high in World War II, well above what it is today. Yet the annualized inflation rate was only 2% for a period of two decades following the war. During the Reagan and Bush administrations of 1981-1992, the inflation rate trended downward even though the debt quadrupled. If there is an upper limit to government debt in terms of its effect on price inflation, it has yet to be experienced.

Official Debt and Public Debt

Congress has divided government spending into two classes, depending on whether it is accounted for *on-budget* or *off-budget*. Most spending, including interest paid on the debt, is on-budget. Spending on programs with dedicated taxes is considered off-budget, the largest being Social Security. The term *unified budget* refers to the combined on-budget and off-budget items. The unqualified terms, *budget deficit* or *budget surplus*, refer to the unified budget.

Accounting Systems for Federal Debt

The budget deficit is the difference between total government spending and total tax revenues. The difference is covered by the sale of Treasury securities to the public, i.e. bills, notes and bonds. The cumulative total of Treasury securities held by the public is the *public debt*. This is the debt on which real interest payments must be made. The public debt may therefore be regarded as the *real* debt.

The *official debt* is the public debt plus what the Treasury owes to government trust funds like the Social Security Trust Fund. That trust fund has been growing because the inflow from FICA taxes plus the interest credited on the trust fund bonds exceeds the outflow for Social Security benefit payments.

How Off-Budget Programs Affect the Debt

Any spending by the government not covered by tax revenues is financed out of receipts from debt securities sold by the Treasury to the public. That means the increase in public debt is the net deficit from both on-budget and off-budget spending. However the official debt is not affected by off-budget spending if there is a positive balance in the off-budget accounts. The official debt rises or falls depending only on the on-budget imbalance. To understand why this is so, consider the following:

Assume an on-budget balance, and determine the effect of an off-budget surplus. That surplus will increase the intra-government debt in the form of special purpose bonds which the Treasury issues to the appropriate trust funds. Since the Treasury has no other use for funds received, the funds will be spent to redeem some public debt. Thus the increase in intra-government debt will be balanced by an equal decrease in the public debt, leaving the official debt unchanged.

Conversely, an off-budget deficit will draw down intra-government debt. With no other source of funds, the Treasury must borrow from the public to redeem trust fund bonds as required to cover the off-budget deficit. Thus the increase in public debt will be balanced by an equal decrease in intra-government debt, again leaving the official debt unchanged.

We have assumed here that all trust funds have positive balances. However when a trust fund is depleted, any further payments on that program can no longer be covered by drawing on the fund. In that case an off-budget deficit will cause an increasing official debt as the Treasury borrows from the public to cover the payments.

The Brief Period of Budget Surplus

For many years prior to 1997, the deficit in the on-budget programs was far larger than the surplus in the off-budget programs. That meant the unified budget was at times in substantial deficit, which was covered by the sale of Treasury bonds to the public.

As the economy improved in the late 1990s, the on-budget programs moved into near budget balance. With the continued surplus in the off-budget programs, the unified budget thus moved into surplus. That allowed some of the Treasury debt to be retired. The recession of 2001 again moved the on-budget programs into large enough deficit to result in unified budget deficit, which is now growing at an unprecedented rate.

Government "Trust Funds"

Social Security benefits, like all other government outlays, must be paid for each year either by taxes or borrowing, i.e. deficit spending. When a federal trust fund is credited with more income than outgo, the trust fund 'balance' increases. Exactly what does that mean?

Writing IOUs to Yourself

In fiscal year 2005, the federal government ran a $364 billion deficit. That means it spent every dollar of tax receipts, plus $364 billion it borrowed from the public. That is, it sold Treasury bills, notes, and bonds to any entity outside the federal government, including domestic individuals and companies, banks, state and local governments, as well as foreign individuals and central banks.

If it spent everything it received and spent an additional $364 billion of borrowed money, how could it ***credit*** a trust fund balance? The answer is: by writing IOUs to itself. That is, the government issued its own securities to itself in that amount. Unlike debt created when it sells securities to outside entities, the bonds that constitute the trust fund 'balances' are neither debts nor assets, rather they are essentially meaningless bookkeeping entries.

Canceling IOUs to Yourself

In the case where a trust fund program spends more than it takes in, the outlays are still funded the same way that all outlays are funded: by tax revenues and borrowing from the public to make up the shortfall. But the trust fund balance is reduced by the amount of the shortfall. What does that mean? It means the federal government cancels debt to itself by 'redeeming' some of the bonds it issued to itself.

Just as I incur no debt by issuing an IOU to myself, neither do I decrease my liabilities or increase my assets by canceling such an IOU. The same is true of the federal government. The government acknowledges this in the FY 1996 budget document entitled ***Analytical Perspectives***, p. 258, where it says:

"These balances are available to finance future benefit payments and other trust fund expenditures—but only in a bookkeeping sense. Unlike the assets of private pension plans, they do not consist of real economic assets that can be drawn down in the future to fund benefits."

When a Trust Fund Balance Reaches Zero

What happens when a trust fund is depleted? ***Nothing***, because the trust fund balance does not pay for program outlays. Current tax receipts and borrowing from the public pay for all program outlays. Future benefit payments must be paid out of future tax collections and borrowing.

Furthermore the amount spent by a program like Social Security is determined by the beneficiary formulas written into the law. Until the formulas are changed by amending the law, the federal government must make good on those obligations. The trust fund balances are irrelevant, both financially and legally.

The Real Meaning of a Government Trust Fund

The very use of the term ***trust fund*** when applied to federal trust funds is misleading. As the government puts it in ***Analytical Perspectives, FY 1996***, p. 251:

"The Federal budget meaning of the term *trust* differs significantly from its private sector usage. In the private sector, the beneficiary of a trust owns the income generated by the trust and usually its assets. A trustee, acting as a fiduciary, manages the trust assets on behalf of the beneficiary. The trustee is required to follow the stipulations of the trust, which he cannot change unilaterally. In contrast, the federal government owns the assets and earning of federal trust funds, and it can raise or lower future trust fund collections and payments, or change the purpose for which the collections are used by changing existing law."

On Budget Deficits

"The national deficit is like a cancer. The sooner we act to restrict it, the healthier our fiscal body will be, and the more promising our future."

—Senator Paul Simon.

"Our nation's wealth is being drained drop by drop because our government continues to mount record deficits. The security of our country depends on the fiscal integrity of our government, and we're throwing it away."

—Senator Warren Rudman.

Warnings of this type are commonplace today. The thought behind them is that some day the government will be unable to service its growing debt, in short that it will become bankrupt. This is based on the mistaken belief that government borrowing is no different from private borrowing. Individuals and firms can indeed borrow their way into bankruptcy. The government cannot, as long as it borrows in the same currency that it creates.

Imaginary Constraints on Government Spending

The fiat money system that replaced the gold-based system in 1933 ended the dependence of government spending on tax revenues. Today the government has just as much money at its disposal when there is a budget deficit as when there is budget surplus. Indeed there is no practical limit to what the government can spend under a fiat money system. The only constraint is self-imposed.

Yet government fiat money is still treated as a scarce economic resource. Congress decides on the affordability of a program based on how much money is projected to be available from taxes or spending cuts. Fiscal responsibility now implies a balanced budget. Some go further and argue that the debt should be retired altogether. That would have a very serious impact on the economy and on the role of the US dollar as the world's reserve currency.

Taxing versus Borrowing

The choice between taxing and borrowing is entirely at the discretion of Congress. That choice does have an economic impact, which can be either good or bad. Unfortunately fiscal policy is based on the belief that deficit spending is ipso facto evil. The real economic consequences are seldom considered in that decision.

When policy makers understand that government deficits present no financial risk, their decisions on spending can be made on the basis of real economic benefits measured against real economic costs. Far too often their focus has been on meaningless accounting issues.

There are times when the attempt to balance the budget can be counter-productive. Deficits are almost unavoidable during recessions. When the economy is sluggish or in recession, deficit spending will usually provide the boost in aggregate demand needed for recovery.

Why the Government Can Always Borrow

Fear that the government will some day be unable to borrow from the public reflects a misunderstanding of the process. Deficit spending creates new bank deposits for the private sector in the amount of that spending. Since reserves earn no interest, banks will normally hold no more than required. However the banking system has no way to dispose of excess reserves except to buy government securities. Thus banks will always be willing to buy risk-free, interest-earning securities offered by the government, up to the limit of their excess reserves. Since the government can pay whatever interest rate the market demands, there will be no shortage of bids from the public for those securities.

More to Think About

Money and Inflation

Price inflation is commonly thought to be caused by "***too much money chasing too few goods***." The general price level is indeed correlated with the money supply, but ***correlation*** should not be confused with ***causation***. In a modern economy, prices are seldom driven by the money supply. More commonly, the money supply reacts to changes in the general price level.

Credit Money versus Commodity Money

It's easy to understand how the money supply can drive prices when a commodity like gold is used as money. In the gold rush days, California was basically on a barter system in which gold traded for goods and services. Gold was an asset for the holder and a liability for no one. As more gold was mined by private enterprise, monetary wealth in California increased. Indeed it increased much faster than the available supply of goods and services, so prices in terms of gold naturally rose.

Gold once comprised the ***monetary base***, but today it is just another commodity. In a modern fiat money system, the monetary base is created by the central bank. However ***base money*** is a minor part of the money supply. Most of the money we use is credit issued by private banks in the form of deposits. Bank deposits are accepted as money because of the promise that they can be converted into base money on demand.

A bank loan increases the money supply but does not increase net wealth. The borrower receives a deposit that he can use as money, but he owes the bank that amount. Thus bank money behaves differently from base money. A bank can issue credit up to a prescribed multiple of its own capital. Within that constraint, the growth of bank money depends only on the demand from the public and the willingness of banks to lend. To understand what causes inflation today, we must therefore determine what creates the demand for credit.

Effects Related to the Price of Credit

The amount of bank money created is a function of many economic variables, including the price of credit which the central bank controls. The central bank can easily increase the price of credit enough to make borrowing unprofitable, stifle growth of the money supply, and even reduce total economic output. That would result in increased unemployment and possibly price deflation.

Conversely the central bank can easily reduce the price of credit, but the results are not symmetric. When the economy is operating well below capacity, cheaper credit will usually increase output without a significant increase in prices up to the point of nearly full employment. Thereafter the effects of cheap credit will generally lead to higher prices.

Demand for Credit and its Effects

The demand for credit arises mainly out of the desire to finance (1) new enterprise, (2) consumer spending, or (3) speculative investment. Let's briefly examine how each of these affects the money supply and prices.

1. A new enterprise or an existing enterprise planning to expand production requires funds well ahead of the expected return from sales. New production is often financed with bank money, and the whole process has little effect on current prices. As the economy grows however, the amount of credit must grow in support. Indeed if credit were curtailed, the economy would stagnate for lack of adequate liquidity.

2. Money borrowed for consumer purchases implies the availability of existing products whose prices have already been set by the sellers. Such borrowing increases the money supply without affecting those prices. However where supply falls short of demand, prices on con-

sumer goods may rise, at least temporarily. But supply shortages tend to occur in isolated cases and are usually short-lived. They seldom have a lasting effect on the general price level.

3. Money borrowed for speculative purposes mainly affects asset prices, particularly stocks and real estate. If the borrowing cost is set too low for an extended period, asset prices can become inflated. This creates a money illusion that can lead to a relaxed attitude by consumers toward higher prices, and result in a general increase in the general price level.

Effects of Government Deficit Spending

Government deficit spending is normally financed by borrowing from the private sector. On balance, such borrowing and spending has no effect on the amount of base money, though it does increase the net financial wealth of the private sector in the form of Treasury securities. However contrary to conventional wisdom, there is no significant correlation between government deficit spending and price inflation.

If the government were unable to obtain funds through taxes or bond sales, it may resort to printing money to spend. If continued long enough, such spending would end in hyperinflation. This occurs infrequently and mainly as a result of serious corruption, revolution, or war. Hyperinflation is quite different in origin and character from the low level inflation that exists in most fiat money systems today.

A Case History—Inflation in the 1970s

During the 1970s, the US experienced a significant inflation in which the consumer price index rose at an annualized rate of 7.5%. However M1 rose relative to the real GDP at an annualized rate of about 3%. Clearly something besides an excess of transaction money drove that inflation.

A major factor was the roughly ten-fold increase in the price of oil resulting from two oil embargoes by OPEC. That led to a sharp increase in material costs in several important industries which had to be passed on as higher consumer prices. However that was not the only important cause of the inflation during the period.

Key industries were dominated by powerful corporations, some of which had the clout to set prices. This in turn enabled strong unions to gain generous wage contracts, sometimes well above the growth in labor productivity. COLAs in the contracts added a positive feedback effect on wage growth. The benefits achieved by unions were mainly in the manufacturing sector, but gradually spread to the service sector.

With labor the main cost in most consumer items, the result was a cost-push inflation that became a serious wage-price spiral. Increasing wages helped enable consumers to absorb the rising prices imposed by producers. However these factors, together with the demands for expanding production, required a larger money supply to support it. As profit-seeking enterprises, banks were more than happy to lend to creditworthy borrowers, and so the money supply grew.

There are numerous forces that apply upward pressure to prices which are not driven by money supply growth. Global competition now limits the power of many domestic producers to set prices. But less competitive sectors still exist and contribute to a long term upward bias in prices. As prices rise, the money supply growth must necessarily keep pace.

Who Benefits from Seigniorage?

During the era of commodity money, the monetary base consisted mainly of precious metal coins minted by the State. The State spent them into circulation for the goods and services it needed. ***Seigniorage*** was the difference between the face value of coins and the cost of producing them, effectively a tax on the public.

The Monetary Base Today

In a modern fiat money system, seigniorage benefits arise in a different way. The monetary base consists mainly of the liabilities of the central bank. In the U.S. the Fed issues its liabilities as Federal Reserve notes and credits held on deposit for banks. Those notes and deposits are different forms of the same liability, and are interchangeable on demand. Since the government accepts only Fed liabilities in payment of taxes, those liabilities are in effect tax credits with no tangible backing. Their wide acceptance as a medium of exchange is based on the power of the government to enforce tax collection.

The cost of producing Federal Reserve notes is very small relative to their face value, which means that seigniorage from issuing them is potentially quite large. However the total amount issued is a function of demand by the public, and not at the discretion of the Fed itself. Because they earn no interest, the public only holds what it needs for use as portable money. The largest demand for Federal Reserve notes comes from those countries where the local currency is not trusted. The Fed estimates that more than half of its notes are now overseas.

Coins comprise only about 1% of the monetary base, and are of minor significance. They are a special case which will be discussed later. Our focus will be mainly on seigniorage from notes, which is quite different from the case of coins.

The Production and Distribution of Notes

The Bureau of Engraving and Printing in the Treasury produces all Federal Reserve Notes. The Fed buys notes at cost, and credits the Treasury's account at the Fed in payment. The Fed offers notes on demand to banks at face value, debiting their accounts at the Fed in payment. Banks offer notes on demand to depositors, debiting their individual accounts in payment. Banks can return notes to the Fed and regain credits in their Fed accounts. Likewise the public can return notes to their banks and gain credits in their accounts.

Seigniorage from Notes

Since the Fed buys notes at cost from the Treasury, it would appear that the Fed gains the seigniorage benefits when it sells them at face value to banks. However as a matter of accounting, the Fed simply swaps liabilities on its balance sheet between note obligations and deposit obligations as it sells and redeems notes with banks. The Fed's capital is not affected, and it gains nothing from exchanges with banks.

Now consider what happens when the public increases its cash holdings by withdrawals from banks. Since a bank's vault cash is part of its reserves, the net withdrawal of cash reduces aggregate banking system reserves. In order to maintain control of the Fed funds rate, the Fed must replenish those reserves. It does so by buying Treasury securities in the open market, a process known as **monetizing the debt**. In effect, the public acquires its cash by selling Treasury securities. Conversely it buys Treasury securities to dispose of its excess cash.

The total value of the notes held by the public is backed by an equal value of Treasury securities held by the Fed. Interest earned on those securities is the main source of income for the Fed. However the Fed, as the issuer of base money, has no need for profits in its own currency. In fact it rebates almost all of its income after expenses to the Treasury. As a result, the Treasury gains nearly interest-free loans in proportion to the notes held by the public. Thus the seigniorage benefit from notes in circulation goes to the Treasury. It is equal to the total interest paid on the Treasury securities in the Fed's portfolio, less the cost of producing the notes and the Fed's cost of distribution.

Seigniorage from Coins

The U.S. Mint, a bureau of the Treasury, produces all circulating coins, and sells them at face value to the Fed. In other respects, the distribution of coins to the public is the same as for notes. Note that the seigniorage for the Treasury from the sale of coins occurs at the time of sale rather than through rebates from the Fed, as with the sale of notes. It is equal to the difference between in the face value of the coins and the cost of their production, basically the same as it would have been in the era of commodity money.

As the Treasury spends its seigniorage profits, aggregate reserves of the banking system would increase. However the Fed must recapture excess reserves in order to maintain control of the Fed funds rate. It does so by selling Treasury securities from its own portfolio, which returns those interest-earning Treasury securities to the public. That increases the interest payments due to the public from the Treasury, which works in the opposite way from note seigniorage. However the value of coin seigniorage is negligible in comparison, and can thus be ignored.

Who is the Real Beneficiary of Seigniorage?

Seigniorage from notes reduces the net interest paid by the Treasury on its debt securities. But the notion that the Treasury itself benefits from the reduction in interest payments on the debt is misleading. It implies the Treasury is a profit-seeking enterprise competing with the public for a piece of the financial pie. Ultimately that would drain bank deposits and the reserves of the banking system, and create a liquidity crisis. The government cannot avoid returning the so-called seigniorage to the private sector in the form of increased spending, lower taxes, or reduced borrowing. *In a modern fiat money system, the seigniorage benefit for the government is an illusion.*

Seigniorage from Foreign Holding of Notes

What about Federal Reserve notes that are bought by foreign interests for use overseas? They too reduce the net interest paid on Treasury debt. Moreover if they never return to the US, they represent a very large gift of seigniorage to the US economy. Whether those notes are purchased in exchange for a foreign currency or acquired by exporting goods to the US, the public as a whole is the beneficiary.

Tax or Borrow?

Suppose the government planned a one-year program to repair the crumbling highway system at a cost of $100 billion. If the Treasury sold securities directly to the Fed to acquire the funds, the Fed would have to soak up most of the spending by selling the securities to the public itself. Otherwise it would lose control of the Fed funds rate. The only truly viable options are taxing or borrowing from the public at market rates.

Implementing the Options

The simplest taxing option would be a one-time surcharge on everyone's tax bill. Based on current tax revenues which total about $2000 billion, that would amount to a 5% surcharge for one year.

The borrowing option would involve the sale of $100 billion in Treasury bonds to the public at an interest rate determined in the market, which we will assume averages 5%. With an otherwise balanced budget, and assuming no increase in tax revenues, additional borrowing would be required to cover the interest payments. In that unlikely case the amount borrowed and interest paid would increase at an annual rate of 5%.

The Common Elements

In both options, the government creates a circulation of financial assets with the public which enables work that would not normally be initiated by private enterprise. The government receives $100 billion from the public. In return the public receives the benefits of the highway repair, and those doing the work receive income of $100 billion paid by the government. The taxes due on that income will cover a portion of the interest payments due to the bond holders in the borrowing option.

Other things equal, the entire $100 billion is paid out as fast as it is collected because the Treasury does not maintain balances in excess of what it needs to cover its near-term obligations. Regardless of how it is funded, the program will result in some redistribution of financial assets. However it is important to note that *all government spending redistributes financial assets within the private sector*.

The Differences

In the taxing option, the government *extracts* the funds in proportion to one's normal tax liabilities. That means most of the cost will be covered by those in the higher taxable income group. In the borrowing option the government obtains the funds on a *voluntary* basis, according to the investment preferences of the public. Again most of the funds come from those with higher taxable incomes because they normally have more loanable funds.

The evidence of a tax payment is a cancelled check. The evidence of a loan is a cancelled check *plus* an interest-bearing Treasury security. The latter can be sold, traded, or pledged as collateral for a loan, and thus has value that the cancelled check does not.

Financial Equivalence of Both Options

Measured in terms of *present value*, both options are equivalent in cost to the public as a whole. In the taxing option, the present value of the money paid up front is obviously $100 billion. In the borrowing option, the present value of the future tax required to retire the debt is also $100 billion. To understand why that is so, consider the following scenario:

With no tax to pay up front, the public could invest the $100 billion in a sinking fund returning 5% per year, the assumed yield on the Treasury bonds. At some future date, if the government chose to pay off that debt, it could levy a one-time tax surcharge, which the sinking fund would fully cover. Thus the $100 billion paid for the sinking fund is equivalent to having paid that amount in taxes up front. Note: ***present value*** does not depend on whether or not the $100 billion was actually invested.

Effects on Wealth Distribution

The taxing option involves no net loss of financial wealth to the private sector. In effect the government merely transfers $100 billion from those who pay the additional taxes to those who receive the income for doing the work. While the two groups are not mutually exclusive, the transfer is mainly from higher income to lower income earners because the former pay the bulk of the taxes and the latter do most of the work.

The borrowing option ***increases*** the financial wealth of the private sector. The funds used to purchase the $100 billion in bonds are returned as payments for the work, and the bonds represent new savings. The interest payment of $5 billion on the bonds is drawn mainly from the higher taxable income group who are also more likely to own the bonds, directly or through intermediaries.

A More Likely Scenario

The two options considered above are opposite extremes for financing the $100 billion program. Some combination of the two is a more likely scenario in a growing economy. The $5 billion interest cost in the borrowing option would require an increase of only 0.25% in total tax revenues. That is well below the growth rate in total tax revenues which normally averages about 5% per year. Thus the funds needed to pay the interest in the borrowing option would likely be available without additional borrowing.

There is one clear argument in favor of borrowing for the highway repair program. The real benefits can be expected to last several decades. To the extent that there are financial inequities across generations, it would be fair to leave some of the costs to later generations who will also enjoy the real benefits.

The Trade Deficit

For over three decades, the U.S. has consistently imported more than it has exported. That automatically increases foreign ownership of U.S. assets, both financial and real. Many view the trade deficit with alarm, and see it as diminishing the wealth of America. They also fear that some day the U.S. will be unable to pay off it indebtedness to foreign interests, or that the exchange value of the dollar will collapse. A closer look will show that these fears are unrealistic.

Investing in America

One nation invests in another by selling to it more than it buys. When an American buys a Japanese-made auto and pays in dollars, the Japanese auto company acquires a dollar balance in a U.S. bank. In so doing, it has invested in the America. If the auto company wanted payment in yen rather than dollars, the buyer would first have to trade his dollars for yen. Then the seller of yen rather than the Japanese auto company would have invested in the America.

Trade Policies

Contrary to conventional wisdom, the U.S. does not seek to borrow from its trading partners to support its trade deficit. Rather the trade deficit reflects the desire of foreigners in the aggregate to increase their holdings of U.S. dollar assets. They willingly offer their goods and services in exchange for dollar credits. They vigorously compete in the U.S. market, selling at the lowest possible prices, while attempting to hold down their domestic wages to increase their competitiveness. When foreign goods are offered at attractive prices in an open economy like that of the U.S., they will be bought in preference to higher-priced U.S. goods of the same quality.

Another reason for the U.S. trade deficit is that its trading partners depend on exports to help support their own domestic employment. As long as other countries promote trade surpluses with tariffs, import restrictions, and interventions in the financial markets to support the U.S. dollar, they are helping foster the U.S. trade deficit. In a truly floating exchange rate system, free of trade restrictions, the U.S. trade deficit would tend towards zero over time.

How Foreigners Can Use Their Dollar Holdings

Foreigners can use their dollar holdings in several ways:

1. They can buy U.S. goods and ship them home for their own use or resale, which will reduce the trade deficit and help support U.S. employment.

2. They can invest them in dollar-denominated assets including new enterprise, which will help support U.S. employment and economic growth.

3. They can trade them for their own or another currency in the forex market, in which case the dollars will simply change hands without affecting net investment in the U.S.

4. They can sell the dollars to their central banks, which will invest them in U.S. Treasury securities and thereby help to hold down long term interest rates.

A Broader View

The U.S. economy comprises not only its domestic base but also the many foreigners who invest in the U.S. one way or another. The greater the fraction of their assets that foreigners hold in dollars, the more their financial well-being depends on a strong dollar. Ultimately they will become full members of the U.S. economy. That they may live overseas is no longer relevant.

Suppose an Italian decides to produce wine for sale in America. He hires workers, develops a vineyard, bottles the wine, and exports it to the U.S. for sale. If his wine sells, the U.S. trade deficit will have increased by the amount of dollars he acquires. One can think of him as an American who happens to work abroad. Like any American citizen, he must pay U.S. taxes on the net income from his sales in America. The wine is produced in Italy, but his earnings are in dollars and they remain a part of the dollar economy.

If his sales do well enough, he will become an integral part of the U.S. economy. His own financial well-being will depend on the strength of the dollar relative to the euro. The stronger the dollar, the more euros he can acquire to cover his employee costs, and therefore the greater his profits in euros. Because of the large market the U.S. presents and the status of the U.S. dollar as world's primary reserve currency, in effect **the U.S. trade deficit expands the dollar economy beyond America's geographic borders.**

Why a Collapse of the Dollar is Unlikely

As long as foreigners run a net trade surplus. with the U.S, their dollar-denominated assets will increase. They can repatriate their dollar holdings individually, but not collectively. A wave of selling dollars would leave the same quantity of dollars in foreign hands, but at a lower value in terms of the foreign currencies. The trade deficit would be largely self-correcting if foreigners collectively tried to repatriate their dollars.

The time will come when some nations have acquired more dollar-denominated assets than they wish to hold. However they cannot arbitrarily cut their exports to the U.S. without increasing their unemployment levels, unless their domestic market can take up the slack. Nations that have accumulated large dollar reserves must also be careful in diversifying into other currencies lest they hurt the dollar's exchange value and shoot themselves in the foot. A collapse of the dollar is highly unlikely short of an environmental catastrophe or runaway inflation that ruins the U.S. economy.

The U.S. trade deficit will likely diminish in relative terms as the economies of its major trading partners grow. But the deficit will continue until they are capable of buying all of their own production. Until then, foreign investment in the U.S. will grow, and further expand the dollar economy and dollar's role as the world's primary reserve currency, a role once played by the British pound sterling.

Counterfeit Money, Who Takes the Hit?

Suppose someone produces perfect counterfeits of subway tokens and uses them to ride on the subway. Who takes the hit? Obviously the subway company does because it will sell fewer tokens as a result. Its net profit will decrease by the price of the subway rides bought by those counterfeit tokens, less the cost of producing them because that reduces the number of tokens it has to produce itself.

A Counterfeit Money Scenario

Now suppose someone produces perfect counterfeits of Federal Reserve notes and spends them into circulation. Is this analogous to the scenario for counterfeit subway tokens? If so, who takes the hit? As we will see, the case of counterfeit notes is quite different and much more complex.

It is virtually impossible to produce perfect counterfeit notes, but some are good enough to circulate for long periods before they are detected. One million dollars worth of counterfeit notes would have an imperceptible effect on the economy. So let's assume an amount large enough to have a measurable effect, say five billion dollars worth. That's only about 1% of the cash in circulation, but more significantly it is about 20% of the cash that banks hold.

What Happens to the Excess Cash?

As the counterfeit notes are spent into circulation, the public will find it has more non-interest-earning cash than it wishes to hold. So it will deposit the excess cash in bank accounts where it adds to vault cash, and thereby increases the aggregate reserves of the banking system. Since banks don't earn interest on cash, they will swap the excess cash for deposits at the Fed in order to lend in the Fed funds market or to purchase interest-earning assets like T-bills.

The Effect of Increased Bank Reserves

The increase in banking system reserves will create an imbalance in supply and demand and apply downward pressure on the Fed funds rate. In order to maintain control of that rate, the Fed will have to soak up the excess reserves by selling some of its own Treasury securities to the public. Thus perfect counterfeit notes spent into circulation will increase the public's holding of Treasury securities, and thereby increase the interest payments due to the public from the Treasury.

Does the Treasury therefore take the hit? No, that implies the Treasury is a profit-seeking enterprise, no different in that respect from the subway company. The Fed is the source of the government money, and Treasury simply recycles what the Fed has previously issued.

Who takes the hit?

In a primitive all-cash economy, counterfeiting would indeed increase the cash in circulation and dilute its value. The holders of cash would then take the hit. But modern economies operate mainly on bank-issued credit, not cash.

The additional interest payments owed to the public by the Treasury resulting from the counterfeit notes must ultimately be covered by increased taxes. That's a wash for the public as a whole, but not for those who pay more in taxes than they receive in interest payments. The net effect is a redistribution of financial wealth within the private sector. It's fair then to conclude that the public takes the hit on counterfeit notes in approximate proportion to the taxes they pay.

The Fed estimates that over one-half of the Federal Reserve notes in circulation have migrated overseas for use as a trusted medium of exchange. It is interesting that if, on balance, genuine Federal Reserve notes return to the domestic economy from overseas, they would have exactly the same effect in the U.S. as would new perfect counterfeit notes.

A Plan for
Monetary Reform

The End of Fractional Reserve Banking

When banks issue loans in a ***fractional reserve system***, they create interest-earning assets for themselves as well as deposits for borrowers. This enables them to control purchasing power in the economy and offer it wherever they choose. Many people think such a system places too much leverage in the hands of private banks. Indeed much of their lending now goes to support speculation in asset price appreciation, which inflates prices, increases the fragility of the financial system, and serves no useful purpose in the real economy.

The apparent solution to these problems is to replace the current system with one requiring fully-backed bank deposits. We will examine a number of issues that must be addressed, and propose a particular system. First we will briefly review the fractional reserve system of the U.S.

Money in a Fractional Reserve System

There are two kinds of money, ***base money*** and ***bank money***. The Fed creates the ***monetary base*** when it purchases Treasury securities from the public. It pays by simply crediting the seller's bank with a deposit at the Fed, while the bank credits the seller with a deposit in his own account. This issue of base money in exchange for Treasury securities is known as ***monetizing the debt***.

Base money consists of currency and bank deposits at the Fed. All payments to and from the government involve the transfer of base money. For example, when one writes a check to pay his taxes, his bank must surrender that much of its *reserves* of base money to the Treasury in order for the check to clear. Bank reserves held on deposit at the Fed are known as *Fed funds*.

Bank money refers to deposits in banks, all of which are claims on base money. The viability of bank money depends on the promise that the bank deposits can be converted on demand into base money. Bank money is created when a bank issues a loan. It does so by simply crediting the borrower's account with a deposit. The bank must hold enough reserves of base money to meet the reserve ratio requirement on its demand deposits.

If necessary, a bank can borrow the reserves it needs in the money market or from another bank. That simply transfers reserves from one bank to another without increasing the total amount in the banking system. If the demand for reserves exceeds the available supply, the interest rate on reserves will increase. That interest rate is known as the *Fed funds rate*. The Fed's primary monetary policy instrument is control of the Fed fund rate. In order to hold the Fed funds rate on its *target rate* the Fed will have to supply additional reserves to meet the demand. Thus an increase in net lending by banks automatically brings forth the additional reserves needed to back them. The ultimate constraint on bank lending is the capital adequacy requirement, not the fractional reserve requirement.

Money in a Fully-Backed System

In a fully-backed system, banks cannot create deposits through lending as they do in a fractional reserve system. All deposits must be matched by reserves of base money at the Fed. However banks can accept deposits of cash or by checks because the reserves backing them accompany the deposit. The total money supply consists of transaction deposits at banks and cash in circulation. Term deposits, such as CDs, represent investments which are not fully-backed, and therefore do not count as a part of the money supply.

Transaction deposits are the equivalent of cash and therefore earn no interest. For income, depositors can purchase Treasury bills, or a variety of short-term investments offered by *private financial institutions (PFIs)*. That includes money market mutual funds which represent shares in short-term debt with checking facilities against that debt. Except for Treasury bills, none of these securities are free of credit risk.

Credit cards are not allowed because they create bank deposits without full backing. However debit cards are acceptable because they simply transfer existing deposits from buyers to sellers. Charge cards are also acceptable because they create private debts of buyers to sellers, but do not create new deposits.

The Dual Role of Banks

Banks as we know them today perform two distinct roles: They are profit-seeking intermediaries as well as depositories. As intermediaries, they provide a link between those with excess funds and those in need of funds, borrowing in order to lend at a profit. As depositories they accept deposits, provide payment facilities, and issue cash on demand in exchange for deposits.

In a fully-backed system, banks could continue to perform both roles. They would have to hold reserves at the Fed to fully back their deposit liabilities. In addition they would need their own liquid assets, sufficient to manage cash flow in their investment activities. Thus a bank would need two separate accounts at the Fed, a *reserve account* and a *liquidity account*. When a bank spends, the Fed would debit the bank's liquidity account and simultaneously credit the reserve account of the seller's bank. The seller would receive a new credit in his own bank account.

The Central Bank as Sole Depository

In a fully-backed system, there are good reasons for transferring the depository role from private banks to the Fed. The functions are basically clerical and offer little opportunity for income other than fees for service.

Banks have less incentive to seek customer deposits when they cannot be used to back the creation of new deposits, as in a fractional reserve system. Since all deposits would be entries in a common computer network, determining balances and clearing checks could be done instantly, thus eliminating checking system float and its logistic complexities. It is worth nothing that when private banks no longer serve as depositories, the concept of bank reserves loses its meaning.

Henceforth, we will assume that the Fed is the sole depository, and refer to its local branches as **banks**. Former banks that remain in business become PFIs along with finance companies, pension funds, mutual funds, insurance companies, and the like. Any economic entity, whether a PFI, a firm, or an individual, may open a transaction account at a local branch of the Fed.

Similarity to Warehouse Banking

A fully-backed system is similar in some respects to warehouse banking, a system that preceded fractional reserve banking. In exchange for a fee, private warehouse banks accepted deposits of precious metal coins for safekeeping in well-guarded vaults, and allowed depositors to make payments by transferring title to the coins rather than by transferring the coins themselves. They did not create deposits through lending.

A key difference is that money now exists as intrinsically worthless notes and coins or entries in a computer, either of which can be increased without limit. For that reason, the issue of money is necessarily a monopoly of the Fed. The size of the money supply depends on the policies of the Fed rather than on private enterprise, as in the era of warehouse banking.

Monetary Policy Options

The basic goal of monetary policy is to provide financial liquidity as needed to support a growing economy while limiting price inflation to some small value. Monetary policy can be implemented in two different ways: (1) control of the money supply growth rate, which leaves the money market interest rate as a residual, or (2) control of the money market interest rate, which leaves the money supply as a residual. The ***money market rate*** is the interest rate at which major PFIs lend money to each other on a short-term basis, say 30 days. It is analogous to the London Inter-Bank Offer Rate (LIBOR) in Eurodollars.

Some economists have advocated option (1) with a fixed growth rate of the base money supply consistent with the potential growth rate of the real economy plus a small inflation rate. A key objection to this is its inflexibility. There are certain to be significant external shocks to the economy from time to time. The negative impact could be lessened with adjustments in interest rates, which a fixed money growth rate policy would not allow. Furthermore the potential growth rate slowly varies for a number of reasons and cannot be accurately forecast.

Option (2) is adopted here because it provides the flexibility to deal with special circumstances. It is also more effective in limiting interest rate volatility. Firms cannot plan efficiently if interest rates vary sharply and unpredictably. Selecting the optimal interest rate to target at any given time is not easy. Mistakes have been made which are usually recognized only in retrospect. However a great deal of experience now exists in many different economies which support the overall effectiveness of the interest rate targeting option.

Monetary Policy Implementation

The Fed steers the money market interest rate toward the target rate through its ***open market operations***. When the interest rate rises above the target rate, the Fed purchases securities in the open market to increase the aggregate supply of deposits. When the interest rate falls below the target rate, the Fed sells securities. In this way it continually adjusts the supply of loanable funds to meet the demand at approximately the target rate.

The normal growth bias of the economy creates the need for an expanding money supply. In order to maintain control of the overnight lending rate, on balance the Fed must purchase securities from the public to support the demand. That means the Fed's portfolio of securities will continue to grow with time.

Financial Capital Formation

PFIs perform a critical role in the economy. They acquire funds from investors which they pool and make available to borrowers. This typically involves selling financial instruments as diverse as debt securities, mutual funds, and insurance policies. As lenders they need to cover their costs and make a reasonable profit in order to stay in business. In the process, private sector debt is created. However the base money supply remains the same unless the Fed acts to change it. In the current fractional reserve system, most of the private sector debt has been generated by PFIs rather than banks. In a fully-backed system, virtually all of the private sector debt would be generated by PFIs.

Dealing with Liquidity Problems

A PFI in good standing may unconditionally borrow from the Fed. The interest rate is set 100 basis points above money market target rate. This large spread means that PFIs will use the lending facility mainly to cover short term cash flow problems, not as a source of funds to invest. The loan must be collateralized by the borrower with Treasury securities. It may be rolled over indefinitely as long as the borrower has sufficient funds on deposit to pay the interest and to cover any change in the market value of the collateral.

The Fed<>Treasury Relationship

The Treasury sells securities to the Fed only to roll over the maturing securities in the Fed's portfolio. Otherwise all new Treasury securities are sold to the public, which ensures that the yields reflect the open market rate. The principal source of income for the Fed is the interest it earns on its

Treasury securities. Periodically, the Fed refunds any income in excess of its operating costs to the Treasury.

The Treasury holds all of its funds on deposit at the Fed, which acts as its banker. In a fully-backed system there is no need for the Treasury to hold deposits at PFIs. However it must manage its cash flow to maintain its average balance at the Fed at some fixed level on average. The purpose is to minimize variations in the private sector money supply, and thus facilitate control of the money market interest rate by the Fed. That means the Treasury must cover its deficit spending with the sale of its securities in a timely manner.

Minimizing the Risk of Systemic Failure

PFIs borrow to lend at a profit, but there are wide variations in cash flow risk due to maturity mismatching of assets and liabilities. Nothing about a fully-backed system would eliminate excessive risk taking by PFIs. To minimize the danger of systemic failure caused by a large default, capital adequacy requirements should be imposed on all PFIs considered *"too large to fail"*. The required capital-to-asset ratio should be an increasing function of the mismatch between their assets and liabilities. Details of the formula will require careful study to ensure its effectiveness and practicability.

There is no need for deposit insurance in a fully-backed a system, and no government insurance should be provided on the financial instruments offered by the PFIs. Bond rating agencies would likely expand their domain to rate the creditworthiness of PFIs as entire institutions. That would be of value to investors. More importantly it would mean institutional creditworthiness was of special importance in the competitive business of lending for a profit.

Advantages of a Fully-Backed System

As proposed, a fully backed system should be more robust than the fractional reserve system. It should also help direct financial resources to more productive activities.

With a single depository, all payments are transfers between accounts within a single bank, which allows for instant clearing, eliminates the nuisance of checking system float, and significantly reduces associated costs.

Other advantages include the elimination of overnight sweeps and other sterile games that banks play to get around the fractional reserve requirement.

Estimating the Base Money Supply

Since money earns no interest, firms and households will hold the minimum required to meet their liquidity needs. Holding money in excess of near-term needs represents a *real* cost in purchasing power equal to the inflation rate, which has averaged about 3 percent over the long term. Alternatively, it represents an opportunity cost which varies with the money market interest rate.

If the fully-backed system were working in the U.S. today (2007), a reasonable estimate of the base money supply would include the currency in circulation ($750 billion), the total of demand deposits and other checkable deposits ($620 billion), and what PFIs would need for liquidity ($380 billion), assumed to be about 4% of total assets of the banking system.

The estimated base money supply would thus total about $1,750 billion. To increase it to that level, the Fed would have to buy about $1,000 billion of the outstanding Treasury securities which now total about $4,500 billion.

Transition to a Fully-Backed System

The transition would not be easy. It would have to be carefully planned and phased in to give all parties adequate time to make the necessary adjustments. Banks and thrifts would have to close out their existing loans, since they represent bank money that is no longer allowed under a fully-backed system. Many bank loans would probably be purchased by other PFIs as investments. Without the depository role, banks would no longer need the same number of branch offices, and would likely sell there excess facilities to the Fed. A logical way to proceed would be to gradually increase the reserve ratio requirement on existing depositories until it reached 100 percent.

About the Author

William Hummel's formal education was in science and engineering. He received a bachelor degree in physics from UC Berkeley and a masters degree in electrical engineering from USC. His professional career was in the field of guided missiles and spacecraft engineering, mainly at Hughes Aircraft Company where he became Chief Scientist of the Controls Laboratory in the Space Systems Division.

During his forty years at Hughes, he was engaged in the design and development of flight control systems for several guided missiles, synchronous orbit communication satellites, and science mission spacecraft. The latter included the Surveyor, which in 1966 was the first spacecraft to soft land on the moon.

His interest in monetary systems and economics developed after he retired in 1990. The impetus came from internet discussion groups and e-mail exchanges with a number of economists. For the last twelve years, much of his time has been spent in the study of macroeconomics as influenced by the social institution we call **money**.

978-0-595-42415-3
0-595-42415-5

Made in the USA
San Bernardino, CA
13 July 2014